One Psalm at a Time

One Psalm at a Time

AMARA KURSHA

Duluth, GA

One Psalm at a Time
Copyright © 2017 Amara Kursha
All rights reserved.

No part of this book may be reproduced or transmitted in any form or by any means, electronic or mechanical, including photocopying, recording or by any information storage and retrieval system, without written permission from the publisher, except for the inclusion of brief quotations in a review.

Address inquiries to the publisher:
The Word Herd
P.O. Box 956324
Duluth, GA 30095

Learn more about the author at:
www.thewordherd.com

ISBN: 978-0-9990909-0-9 (print)
ISBN: 978-0-9990909-1-6 (ebook)

Library of Congress Control Number: 2017950523

Printed in the United States of America

Acknowledgements

First and foremost, I would like to take this opportunity to thank my Lord and Savior Jesus Christ for being the true inspiration behind this collection of poems. Not a day goes by that I do not thank Him for His love and for His guidance. He is worthy to be praised and I am honored to share with the world just how He has helped to change my life. And most importantly, I am honored to call Him my friend.

From the bottom of my heart, I would like to thank my family for being my support system throughout this journey of writing. You three saw the gift within me long before I did, and I honestly cannot thank you enough for believing in me and for being my biggest fans.

I would also like to thank my pastor and my church family at New Destiny Christian Ministries for encouraging me to take that leap of faith and to put my God-given gift on display. You guys allowed me to stand before you week after week for two years just to recite my poetry, and I am more than grateful for the opportunities that have arisen since you blessed me with the opportunity to grace the stage.

To my friends, I would like to say thank you for your help in motivating me to just get the job done. Melvina, you were truly essential to the completion of this book.

Your input was profound, and I just thank you for your contribution. Michelle, your desire to see me as a published author pushed me stretch my vision as a writer, and you honestly made me believe that I could do this.

Lastly, to the reader, I would like to thank you for your interest in wanting to read *One Psalm at a Time*. Your aspiration brings more joy to my heart than you could know. I appreciate you and your contribution to making this dream become a reality. With all sincerity, I thank you.

Table of Contents

I Know Why the Sea Runs Deep 9
These Things 10
I Was Forgiven 13
Psalms 23 14
My Bible 17
I Was Chosen 20
Your Time is Your Life 22
My War Room 23
Adversity 25
Weather the Storm 27
Try Jesus 29
Prayer 30
He Knew Me 32
Godfidence 34
Ask Seek and Knock 36
Footprints 38
Your Will Be Done 40
Deliver Us 42
Goodness and Mercy 44
Psalms 1 46
Obedience 48
Wisdom 50
Have Faith 52
God's Timing 54
Open Letter to Jesus: Eternal Valentine 56

Freedom	58
Testimony	60
Reality Check	62
J.O.B	64
God's Payroll	67
Telephone	69
Service Over Status	71
Battlefield	73
God's Not Finished with Me Yet	75
Eternal Joy	77
Enough	79
God is Love	81
God is in Control	83
He Makes No Mistakes	85
His Voice	87
Trust	89
Church	91
Come as You Are	93
God's Waiting Room	95
Humanity	97
God Is...	99
My Best Friend	102
Fear	103
Decisions, Decisions	105
The Road to Righteousness	107
To Die For	109
Next Chapter	111

I Know Why the Sea Runs Deep

I know why the sea runs deep,
Because it's filled with our lies and the truths we keep.
See, it knows what we know and the things we sweep
Under the rug like we dug to get things we reap.
Now ain't that deep?
Like the words we speak
Never comprehend the meaning,
Until the well runs bleak.
Yea, you think you sleek,
Through every trough and peak.
But I assure, it'll come ashore
And make those knees go weak.
And you'll be asking, "How?"
But those knees will bow.
Before Him as we know it
You'll be screaming,
"Thou! Art My Lord and Savior
My light and only love!
The truth, your name is Jesus,
The one I'm thinking of!
You laid your life for thee
For each and every sin!
Your blood, it covers me
And now you dwell within!"

These Things

If one plus one equals two,
Then what equals you
Minus your possessions?

Are you still the same?
Does your foundation still remain?
Or are they proof of your progressions?

Do these things make you whole;
Make you greater than your self-known expressions
Or do they reflect nothing more than a fraction
Of your self-grown oppressions?
These obsessions.

Do they multiply, or do they divide?
Do they provide a sense of grace
Or do they provide a sense of pride?

Do they reside, in the place we know so well?
The place with hidden chambers,
The place where God should only dwell.

Have they denied,
Your sins of their remission?
Would they die for you today
Or must you ask for their permission?

In addition,
Who owns what
And who owns who?
How can you say you
Own things,
When your things say they own you?

Which is true?
Do you value faith
And do you value favor,
Or do you value Drake
On his worst behavior?
Who gives you life,
God or "B"?
Who follows you and follows me?
DTLR ain't up to par
And Jordans can't make you fly.
That Dior, is not for sure.
Yet, for these things you choose to die.

The question's,
"Why, do you value things more than life
And cause yourself internal strife?"
You know it's wrong
So, make it right.

You see these things?
These things, I now repeat
Will never ever fill that void
And your need to feel complete.
Only God deserves your love;
So, from these things
You must retreat
They can't compete.

I Was Forgiven

My soul caught an infection
Trying to claim it reached perfection
Knowing the lies I kept within,
And knowing that I was born to sin.

It started to spread from limb to limb
Displaying the truth of where I've been.
And showing the facts, no words to say.
Exposing my tainted DNA.

Under the scope
There was no hope
For this disease, in time
Had hit its prime.

Before I knew it, I was dead
No more tears left here to shed
My broken soul, it needed healing
And God's protection from my dealings.

Then I confessed, and was forgiven
I was renewed and now I'm risen.
He saved my life from this infection
And saw His love through resurrection.

Psalms 23

The Lord is my Shepherd
He made me His anomaly
I shall not want
For His word is written homily.

He makes me to lie
Even when I'm standing
Down in green pastures
For His understanding.

He leads me
Though I'm slow to follow
Beside the still waters
Often hard to swallow.

He restores my soul
He knows I'm worth it
He leads me in the paths
Knowing I'm not perfect.

Of righteousness
For His name's sake
I praise Him through the battles
For my life's at stake.

Yea though I walk
With my head held high
Through the valley of the shadow of death
I'll tearfully cry.

I will fear no evil
For you are with me
Jesus, the redeemer
Came to set me free.

Your rod and your staff
They comfort me
In the moments
When the devil won't let me be.

You prepare a table
Despite the distant memories
Before me now,
In the presence of my enemies.

You anoint my head
Provide me closure
With oil
My cup runs over.

Amara Kursha

Surely Goodness
Can heal my strife
And Mercy shall follow me
All the days of my life.
And I will dwell
With love and pleasure
In the house of the Lord
Now and forever.

My Bible

To God
Be the glory
To the author
Of this story

Front to back
Tip to spine
Filled with pages
Of divine

Spoken treasures
All are true
Said by plenty
Known by few

Simple message
Deeper meaning
Through His words
Our heart's He's cleaning

Cleansing now
Our tears and sorrow
For He knows
Our plans tomorrow

Amara Kursha

Plans for good
No harm, no shame
We praise Him so
In Jesus name

Now we may fall
And we may weep
But every shepherd
Knows his sheep

He left behind
Word and protection
For the ultimate
Connection

To God
Be the glory
To the author
Of this story

Back to front
Old to New
Saving souls
From me to you

Simple message
Deeper meaning
Through His words
Our heart's He's cleaning
Then, today and forever
He'll be the same
We praise Him now
In Jesus name.

Amara Kursha

I Was Chosen

I'm not common to the average
Yet, I'm common for my sin
My Savior sees me different
Through my qualities within

He knows my hidden talents
In my soul, He birthed a seed
He saw me as a flower
When at heart, I felt a weed

Blooming with potential
He breathed purpose and a mission
In my life, He opened doors
And then He granted me remission

He saw me like His chosen Shepherd
I was a slave and a deceiver
Like Moses, Joseph and Jacob
And from them He made believers

Matthew, Mary and Luke
Ezra, Hannah and David
Each of us imperfect
But His love has never faded

He picked me from the many
Esther, Peter and Paul
He qualified my blessings
And my name He chose to call

I was chosen.

Amara Kursha

Your Time is Your Life

Ticking are the moments
That we squander night and day
Gone are the hours spent on pleasure
None left to pray.

Zooming are the weeks
Unremembered, with no fear
We lose more than just our meaning
We lose another year.

More precious than our money
More valuable than our things
No feeling can compare
To the joy this present brings.

And when God soon calls to question
Our lives and every chime
I hope you have an answer
I hope you found the time.

My War Room

It was once a tiny space
The perfect place to hide
My things and pride
Deep inside
My war room:
Are words I share in prayers
Above
Tears I shed
With care and love.
Thoughts, I spill
On pen and pad
And Psalms my heart
Is thinking of.

In my war room
I fight.
I fight against,
Not flesh and blood
But spirits known
To kill and flood
Evil plans across the mind
Scriptures on the walls
You'll find.

In my war room,
I trust.

Amara Kursha

I trust Him
Proverbs 3:5
I trust He knows
What sinners do
I trust His word
I know it's true.
So, I pray for me
And pray for you,
In my war room

Adversity

Adversity is the crucible
Of greatness
Full of setbacks, let downs
And we may hate this

But His purpose
Is designed to take us higher.
For good,
He's got to take us through the fire.

Because He's testing,
Everything we thought we knew.
It's on your mind?
Well just don't let it take your view.
He brought you here,
Now let Him work to bring you through.
Broke you down, to build you up
And make you so brand new.

It's a blessing,
Don't take it less than that.
Our lessons are to be learned
With a big impact

So, when it happens
It's not meant for satisfaction.
And the results,
Boil down to your reaction.

Weather the Storm

Like a boat pushing forward,
Against the forces of the tide,
Is your journey deep with purpose
And your mission deep inside.

Your vision may be foggy
Your thoughts, they could be grey.
Your boat could rock
Your faith could stop,
But please don't go astray.

Your problems may be deep
And your fears, they could be vast
But this current's not your future
Because this current will not last.

I promise there'll be thunder
I promise there'll be rain
I promise there'll be lightning
I promise there'll be pain.

I promise it'll be worth it.
I know this to be true.
My boat had rocked
My faith had stopped
I know this could be you.

Amara Kursha

Whether it's the weather,
Or your life in truest form
Just know how big your God is
Don't fret about the storm.

Try Jesus

When your trust has been broken
Heart gone unspoken
And life isn't fair
Try Jesus

When you're down and start to wonder
And the devil starts to plunder
And no one seems to care
Try Jesus

When you're shattered into pieces
Feel like zero, no increases
And you're hurt beyond repair
Try Jesus

Why must you try?
Because for you he chose to die,

He took blow after blow,
So, for the Father you could know.

For your sins, He paid the cost.
And for that bridge, He bore the cross.

And through your bad he's always there,
Just call on him in your despair.

Try Jesus

Amara Kursha

Prayer

Heavenly Father
If you can hear me,
I pray for love,
And hope that you can clearly

See that
We've been trying,
Though our faith is
Slowing dying.

In the midst of
All this terror,
I know with you
There is no error.

I pray for peace
Across the land.
I pray we finally
Take a stand.

Stand together
And unite as one.
Father, let
Your will be done.

In the hearts
Of those to blame
I pray this now
In Jesus name.

Amen.

He Knew Me

Long before my parents knew
Long before my birth was due
Long before my eyes were blue
He knew me

He knew the hairs
Upon my head
He knew the count
That's what He said
He gives me now
My daily bread
He knew me

He knew me like
My dearest friend
He knew I'd love Him
Til' the end
For me His son He
Chose to send
He knew me

He knew I had a
Gift to write
He knew I had the
Will to fight

He knew that I'd
Do what was right
He knew me

I know Him now
Like He knew me
I know His word
It's plain to see
My love for God
Was meant to be
Because He knew me.

Godfidence

What I have is something special
It holds much value, but has no price
This wonder can't be bought or sold
It's tough, but also nice.

It's patient, kind and loving
Slow to take and quick to give
It's full of faith and worth the wait
It taught me how to live.

It helped transform my thinking
And decipher wrong from right
Taught me how to love myself
And to not give up the fight.

Renewed my sense of purpose
Showed me things I failed to see
It taught me to surrender all
To become a better me.

Without it I feel nothing
I take it to work and pray
It gives me strength to carry on
It always brightens up my day.

It's nothing close to average
It raised my awareness and competence
I walk now slowly and hold my head boldly
Because what I have is Godfidence.

Ask Seek and Knock

Asking for us to know Him
Seeking a connection from above
Knocking at our hearts with a constant beat
Beating the rhythm of love

God longs for our affection
He gave us direction and a book
But when staring at the fork in the road
The wrong path is the one that we took.

He never promised life would be easy
But with free will, we made our decision
His light is strong and He showed us the way
But our sins have clouded our vision.

He knew we'd never be perfect
But our souls, He wanted to bless
See our lives can change with just one prayer
But first we must confess.

Then ask for His forgiveness
Seek for His wisdom, His love, His face!
Knock on the door of His Kingdom in heaven
Until we have mercy and grace.

All He wants is a relationship
One special, pure, and complete
Nothing consisting of worldly conditions
We know that could never compete.

We must surrender all our troubles
Deny our flesh and all that's near it
Give glory to Him, with our pride to the side
And be filled with the Holy Spirit.

Because He's asking for us to know Him
And seeking a connection from above
God is knocking at your heart like a heartbeat
Beating the rhythm of love.

Footprints

I was once lost in the trenches of my trials
Blinded by a whirlwind of shame
After shaking my shackles of worry and doubt
I was still burdened by lashes and pain.

Tossed to the side like garbage
Injected with fear and strife
Dodging bullets of enemy power
I was running, running for my life.

Trouble was my past and present
Its touch I knew too well
I tried to control what was out of my hands
And that was the moment I fell.

My God, He said He'd save me
And that this burden wasn't mine
He didn't come when I wanted Him to
But he was surely right on time

My God, He said He loves me
And this I've always known
In my times of suffering
I was never all alone

Looking back at my journey
And where I used to be
There could only be one set of footprints
Because it was then that He carried me.

Amara Kursha

Your Will Be Done

Lord, the world is empty,
And it's open like a blank state.
Yet, it's filled with pain, hurt and hate

Calling souls to its core
Wanting us to just explore it
I witnessed all its damage, but it begged me to ignore it.

And in time I was convinced,
Its ways were justifiable.
When in fact, the world was unreliable.

I had forgotten who provided,
Well before this life of sin.
You blessed me with your Holy Spirit, living right within.

Then I saw the world for what it was,
I didn't need it, not completely.
Its people, things, and money can't complete me.

Now I'm hooked onto your truth
And to your word, I am devoted.
I'm locked into your power and in your strength, I'm fully loaded.

I was long gone; you saved me.
I was spiritually dead.
You let not my will, but your will be done instead.

Deliver Us

Liberation will only come
The day we choose
To put temptation behind us
And to not let it bind us
To the roots of this earth

Left unchanged
It will begin to define us
And each day it reminds us
Of our diminishing worth

If Heaven is where we aim to be
We must first believe
Before we receive
Christ our Savior

Then let go
Of this sinful possession
Pray with confession,
And for changed behavior.

And with boldness
Ask for protection
From the devil's rejection
Unrelenting

Beg and plead
For manna fresh
And strength for the flesh
Way past repenting

Establish a foundation
In his word
And join His herd
Without a fuss

Choose His love
Again, and again
And it is then
He will deliver us.

Amara Kursha

Goodness and Mercy

In their pursuit
To find us
Is God's goodness
And mercy.

Like two angels
Broad in strength
Equipped with love and favor
Of the Most High
Fighting our battles and still
Trying to keep a close eye
On you and me.

See, God is bent on
Blessing and de-stressing our situation
Showing why His goodness and mercy
Will always be a thing of continuation.

We need them daily
They give us hope
And a certain will to push
They show His love
And with every sacrifice
There's a ram stuck in the bush.

We shall not fear
For He's with us
As it's written
In Psalms 23
His goodness and mercy
Will forever follow you and me.

Psalms 1

Blessed is the man
Wise enough to understand
To walk not in the counsel of the ungodly.
Nor stand in the path of sinners
But to surround himself with winners
That choose to submit and admit to God broadly.

Nor sit in the seat of the scornful
For His soul would be weak and mournful.
His heart, hanging from a thread of cord
He would be doomed with no protection
Feeling the wrath of God's rejection.
But His delight, is in the light of the Lord.

And in His law, He meditates day and night
Making sure, no matter what, that he gets it right.
He shall be planted by the rivers of water.
To bring forth its fruit in its season
And to fulfill his purpose and reason.
For He is clay, and God's the master potter.

A tree, whose leaf shall not wither
This man shall not fall or ever quiver
And whatever He does shall prosper, for all to see.
The ungodly aren't righteous, so they don't obey,
But are like the chaff, which the wind drives away.
Losing sight and hope in all they were called to be.

They delight in destruction
And don't give credit
Where credit is due
Therefore, the ungodly shall not stand in the judgment
For they'll never know love or its abundance
In the eyes of the Lord
Or be souls that He once knew

Nor sinners in the congregation
Of the righteous
For the Lord knows the way
Of the righteous
He righteously knows
From His sacred Point of View
But the way of the ungodly shall perish
And those who love Him now
He'll cherish. Which will it be?
The choice is up to you.

Obedience

Blinded by distractions
Burdened by our worry
Muffled praises here and there
Praying in a hurry.

Homeless? Here's a dollar.
Tithing? Maybe two.
I think I've heard that verse before,
I only know a few.

I go to church on Sundays
To my purpose, I've submitted
We do a lot of talking,
But are we really that committed?

Do we know His 10 commandments?
Find the time to love and pray
Think of someone but ourselves
Listen and obey.

Starve our hungry sorrows
Sow into our own salvation
Build despite what others think
An eternal reputation.

There comes a time to wonder
Are we living just to live?
According to His will and plans
Our lives we'll have to give.

It's true we must be willing
No need for pressure or expedience
But know He rewards the righteous
And those who walk in obedience.

Wisdom

Knowledge equals power
Yet only if it's applied
Instructions are solely given
To those who listen and then abide.

The wise thirst for knowledge
The simple feed for trash
The good seek for guidance
While the foolish seek for cash.

The blessed are calm and humble
A fool lives only for pleasure
The godly walk with grace
While the wicked fall forever

The righteous knows their Father
The ruthless lack respect
The gracious give their all
While the selfish choose neglect

Time will kill us slowly
But pride would kill us faster
Repression with no confession
Is a setup for disaster.

The rules are plain as ever
Just truth with no disguise
Fear of God is the foundation
The foundation of the wise.

Have Faith

Expect the unexpected
In this world full of clones
As wolves in sheep's clothing
Too fast to cast stones

The hate is too strong
Step back and see
The devil doesn't want us happy
Not you, nor me

So, what will it be?
Him or thee?
Submit to this oppression
Or do we break free?

Faith is the key
And God is the locket
The plans He has in store
No man on earth can block it

No demon can stop it
Our lives are blessed
No need for us to worry
Or to be so stressed

Let's give it our best
And ignore the hate
Our only job now is
To just Have faith.

God's Timing

It doesn't tick the way
We'd expect it
It doesn't tock when
We want it to go
Sometimes it stalls
In the moment
To teach us patience
In order to grow.

In days, it created
The heavens
For years it has roamed
The earth
It aligns with our gifts
And purposes
And it assigned
Our date of birth.

For a second
We can't doubt its power
Not a minute
Goes by unseen
Hour by hour
It works
Nonstop
For the righteous
And unclean.

No human knows
The answers
For the where, what
When, or who
We only know
It's happening
Right now for
Me and you.

We'll never know
The process
No need for constant
Whining
It'll all unfold
Before our eyes
If we just trust in
His perfect timing.

Amara Kursha

Open Letter to Jesus: Eternal Valentine

At first, I didn't know you
I only knew what people said
I thought I knew the answers
Believed their words and what I read

In time, I'd know the truth
The truth about your name
The truth about your love
And I'd never be the same

I thought my life was over
I thought my life was through
I ended what was love
But found my way to you

I thought there was no other
Who could ever want me?
Damaged, broken, full of it
And blind as I could be

But you took my heart and held it
Held on to every tear
Mended what was loose
Erased my every fear

You listened to my pain
Replaced it with your word
And now I live by what I feel
And not by what I've heard

Your touch is now embedded
In the chambers of my heart
And when I speak of love
I know just where to start

You died for my protection
You died so I could live
Beyond the resurrection
You're the reason that I give

I give this written statement
To say that I am free
That I'm grateful that I prayed to you that night
And got down on bended knee

I'm thankful for your presence
We found each other just in time.
Dear Jesus, you're my savior
And my Eternal Valentine.

Amara Kursha

Freedom

Freedom
A beautiful disaster
Confusion in the mind
Between the servant and the master

Where is it?
This will we call free?
If we all did what we want,
Tell me how would life be?

See, could you
Move with no direction
Fight off every battle
And provide your own protection?

And be righteous
On your own
Succeed with no lead
And take credit all alone

No, we're too human
In our being
That's why having faith is so
Ultimately freeing

Believing isn't seeing
A God that we could touch
But knowing there's a God
That don't require much

But we would rather
Take a stand
Feed into temptation
Ignore His first command

No need to understand
His will because it's perfect
In this life we will never be
But follow Him, because it's worth it

It is worth it,
Being free
Freedom is not meant
To please you or me

Freedom isn't money or fame
Health or expedience
Freedom isn't free
Because it's in obedience

Amara Kursha

Testimony

Shout it in the midst of silence
Live it in a way that speaks
Let it echo in a way that rolls off the tongue
And avalanches from mountain peaks

Give it to a nonbeliever
Give it to the weak and strong
Feed it to the empty
To those who live with plenty
And to the hearts that know right
But, instead, do wrong

Sing it for the common sinner
Belt it from your core and soul
Profess your decision
To walk in God's vision
And how His love
Can make anyone whole

Don't run from their responses
At times they won't agree
Just know inside
That they're filled with pride
And it's your truth
That may set them free

So be sure that you
Are firm in your belief
Never be ashamed
To tell the world your story
Because you live for God, not man
And to Him you give the glory

So, when the moment is presented
Don't fear the proud, rude, or phony
Just pick up that mic, Jesus-like
And tell all your testimony.

Amara Kursha

Reality Check

Who are you afraid of?
Tell me what is it that you fear?
Is the goal to grow?
Or is this just for show?
Because you look like you did last year.

Save me your excuses
The world has just enough
Of those like you
Who know what to do
But complain, when life gets tough.

Tell me, who's your savior?
Tell me, who's your God.
Has He not worked through you?
And then brought you through?
Or was that all just some façade?

Tell me, is it worth it?
Your faith you forsake
Your goals on hold
Your dreams untold
They weren't given to you by mistake.

So, tell me, what would you do
If you knew you couldn't fail?

And knew deep at heart
That from the start
You're the head and not the tail.

Would you leap into God's favor?
Walk on water by His grace?
Preach His word
To souls of many?
Testify and seek His face?

No matter what you choose to do
Don't look back or hesitate
Keep your eyes on the prize
And a word from the wise
"Just step out on faith and elevate!"

Amara Kursha

J.O.B.

Life is just for a season
And we question "why?"
The reason can't just be
Work, pay bills, and die

The reason is far greater
Than the eye can see
In the hands of the creator
It will always be

We have a job
No forms, no application
Learn, reach, turn, preach
Before evaluation

It's about duplication
And saving souls
In addition to you fulfilling
Your dreams and goals

Why me?
Better yet, why not?
There's a billion others praying
Just to have my spot

Just to have one shot
To praise His name
Confess, repent
Hoping not to be the same

This is not a game
We know what to do
The workload is heavy
And the deadline is due

We're some of few
On His missions crew
To seek, find, and help
Those like us too

So, tell me who?
Who will you be?
A servant of God
Or just another employee?

Don't focus on your position
And your limitations
Just look up to God
And exceed His expectations

Amara Kursha

We've got it
If only we tried
Remember your Savior
And remember why He died

Let's get it together
We've been set free
Because working for God
Is not your average J.O.B.

God's Payroll

When your boss is out of raises
Your wallet's out of wages
That check book out of pages
And rent is due.

When you're down to just a twenty
Your bills are more than many
And you scraped up every penny
What do you do?

Do you fix it all alone?
Sell your title for a loan?
Give up everything you own
Or just give in?

Do you find job number three?
Go back to get your degree?
Or quit beyond what the eye can see,
Where you can't win?

You must know to stay alive
There's more to life than a 9 to 5
And through our God, that you can strive
For something more.

No job on earth
Can pay your worth
And from conception to your birth
Your purpose was just in store

So, take your purpose and believe
That in time you will receive
What God will have you to achieve
Within in this war.

And in this life, you were assigned
To seek the truth and you will find
That you weren't broke, it was just your mind
And your faith was poor.

See, God knows all that you've desired
He has a position, where you've been hired
And in this position, you can't be fired
Because He's in control

See, He's into giving raises
Giving love and taking praises
And you'll never again worry about wages
On God's payroll.

Telephone

We all have one
Some have two
Some of them still flip
And some brand new

But when some problems hit
And you're all alone
I wonder who you're calling
On that telephone

See there's nothing wrong with counsel
Or needing a friend
Or needing to vent problems
Every now and again

But who can truly help us,
But our God, the Most High?
Who we can call free
No Data nor Wi-Fi

His calls aren't long distance
'Cause He's always near
His line is always open
'Cause He's always here

Amara Kursha

Here for you, here for me
Yes, for us all.
All we have to do is
Just make that call.

And we all have His number
Yes, the number
Is for heaven
It's 1-800-333-2407.

And it may have been a minute
Or been a while
But it's time we add God
To our speed dial.

Now we all have one
Some have two
Some of them still flip
And some brand new

But when those problems hit
And I'm all alone
I know who I'm calling
On my telephone.

Service Over Status

If God asked us to sell
Our every possession,
Our household and gold
And our little obsessions

For a promise made in heaven
For so much more
Would our faith be rich
Or made poor?

The answers are fairly simple
Who's on top?
God, the Father
Or that bank roll knot?

Tell me who's the master?
We can't have two
In the eye of God's needle
Will the camel get through?

I mean what would we do,
With our freedom of choice?
Follow the crowd
Or listen to the sound of His voice?

Amara Kursha

Lose our money, title, things
All in a blink
I guess we really care
What people think?

And the truth lies in faith
Of the things not seen
There's more to life than
Silver, gold, commas, and green

But the question's been asked
Now it's time for decision
Do we lose ourselves
Or seek God for our provision?

If God asked me to sell
My every possession,
My household and gold
And my little obsessions

For a promise made in heaven
For so much more
I rather be heavenly rich,
Than spiritually poor.

Battlefield

Shots, smoke, fire
Sweat and heat
Pain filled lungs
The smell of defeat

Swords aimed high
While the guns aim low
We're in the midst of the struggle
So, it's READY, SET, GO!

We're at WAR!
Against the things unseen
Violating and perpetrating
Just to snatch our dreams

It is what it seems
Not of flesh and bones
Principalities and thieves
All up through our homes

We're in the zone
Of the deep unknown
Satan thinking that He can come
And take God's throne.

The greatest eternal war
That we've already won,
But we still have to fight
Until it's done.

So, be strong in the Lord
And in His power and might
Put on His whole armor
And be ready to fight

With the helmet of salvation
The shoes of peace
That guide us in love
As our souls increase

The righteousness breastplate
The sword of spirit
The belt of God's truth
We just have to be near it

So, step up in faith
And don't forget that shield
Because we're standing in the middle
Of the battlefield.

God's Not Finished with Me Yet

"For Sale", reads the sign
Of the divine
Things God's replacing within me.

He has me under construction
Increasing His workload production
So, I can live an eternal life sin free.

He sees me beyond the rubble
Of my past pain, hurt, and trouble.
And my imperfections, that are far from sweet.

It's my structure that He's changing
And my heart He's rearranging
To lay His foundation made of concrete.

This new spiritual home,
With Jesus at the cornerstone
Is truly a gift I did not earn.

Jesus wept for me
And paid the debt for me
So that my faults would not leave me to burn.

Amara Kursha

Honestly, I should be gone and dead
For things I've done and for the things I've said
But He kept me

He chose to save my soul
And to make me whole
Promising to never neglect me

I'm human and I make mistakes
And I have what it takes
To overcome this guilt and regret

And I'm thankful for
His love and more
Because, God's not finished with me yet.

Eternal Joy

Happiness
A temporary descendant
That's dependent on circumstance.
And through every instance,
From one to ten,
We fight for this feeling
Again and again.

But why?
Why do we settle?
Settle for money, people, things and shiny metal
Settle to be happy,
In things that rip, die, tear, and rust.
Tell me, is it really in God that we trust?

Must we
Seek for another solution;
A substitution
To feed
Our guilty need
Of this mental pollution?

Or can we
Put these things aside
And look deep inside
For something permanent

Amara Kursha

Nothing turbulent
But stable
Lord knows we're able.

Repent to be able to be content herein
And learn that true happiness comes from within.
We win when we choose not to settle for things;
But instead, trust in God and in the hope He brings.
And avoid by all means the devil's ploy to destroy
It's only then that we'll have eternal joy.

Enough

Acceptance, I use to yearn
For your attention,
I conformed to this world
For just a piece of your retention.

You're my personal invention,
A product of my mind.
I thought in the pieces of your presence
Was myself that I could find.

The self that God created
Not this person that's unsure
Not this shadow in the mirror
But the real me that is pure.

I must have missed the lesson
I must have missed the signs
I memorized His words
But never read between the lines

The devil had me fooled
I was chasing people, things and stuff
Had me feeling that without them all,
I'd never be enough.

But I learned that all that's good and pure
Is tested through the fire
And I passed my test, to testify,
The devil is a liar.

Don't believe his wicked schemes
Or his lies to make you fail
Just pass him by with your head held high
Because through God you will prevail

This is a lesson I had learned
And a truth I fought for many years
Its presence provoked my inner evil
And displayed my deepest fears.

But today I stand myself
A shining diamond in the rough
I know I won't be perfect,
But I now know I am ENOUGH!

God is Love

In the beginning
God created our heaven and home
Orchestrated our existence
And made us his own.

Manufactured our reflections
An image of Him
And in the midst of our rejections
Forgiven our sins.

Slow to anger, patient, gracious
And quick to give.
Powerful, Holy, Faithful
Our reason to live

Our Alpha and our Omega
Beginning and end
We call Him Father
And our best friend

Our miracle living water
Who sent his flood
And in return sent His son
Sealed in His blood

Amara Kursha

His covenant covered rainbows
Fill our skies
And a soul that lives for Him
Never dies

El Shaddai, Jehovah
Yahweh-Shalom
No matter what we call Him
We're never alone

Elohim, our creator
Our life from above
He gives us purpose, peace,
Hope and His love

And His love is truly different
One of a kind
It surpasses every meaning
Any human can find

Unconditional in nature
He loves what is His
We don't deserve it
But it's just who He is.

God is in Control

When trouble knows your number
And it's blowing up your phone
When trials and tribulations
Just can't seem to leave you alone
When sin has grown attached to you
And your soul is under attack
I know you know, the God I know
That always has your back.

When all the world is twisted
And evil likes to shine
When all the bills and rent is due
But you barely made a dime
When you've given your all
And it seems your life is down to nothing
I know you know, the God I know
Is always up to something.

When love is lost and family die
And your heart is filled with fear
When doubt creeps in, and you think within,
"Will I make it through this year?"
When you're tired beyond measure
And you have no strength to pray
I know you know, the God I know
Will always make a way.

Amara Kursha

For He is God, and He alone
Has power in His hands
He can pause and play, rewind and stop
According to His plans.
He holds the key to eternity,
And knows the path of every soul
No need to question life
Because God is in control.

He Makes No Mistakes

The Lord of all creation
Spirit, Father, Son
The King of our salvation
Author of our faith, until He's done
Blew breath into our lungs
And now He soon awaits
His will be done, for everyone
For He makes no mistakes.

Meticulous in measure
Precision to a "T"
He took His time
With us in mind
For all eternity.

He knows our every thought
And on our heads our every hair
His love for us is limitless
No feeling can compare
Our future is His present
Our past, somewhere behind
Our problems may be many
But by these things we're not defined.

His plans are not our plans
His will is not our will
But by every blemish, trial, and hurt
Through our lives He will fulfill
His purposes intended
For all across the land
It may not be what we expected
But the world in His hands.

The Lord of all creation
Spirt, Father, Son
The King of our salvation
Author of our faith, until He's done
Blew breath into our lungs
And now He soon awaits
His will be done, for everyone
For He makes no mistakes.

His Voice

Back when I knew nothing,
Before my soul was bred,
I seldom paid attention
To the voice way in my head.

I blindly led myself
And all who chose to listen.
Claiming to have power,
When in fact that's God's position.

I thought I had the answers,
As blatant as can be.
I fought His words and denied the truth.
Then He chose to humble me.

And I gave my life to Christ,
Confessed of every sin.
And I searched and searched, but could not find
That voice somewhere within.

Then I learned, He's always speaking
His voice so soft and clear.
To His listening sheep, who learn to trust,
His voice and truly hear.

Amara Kursha

For we must tune out the world
And clear our minds as His believers
Be still for just a moment
And change the dial on our receivers

Reposition our antenna's
For this privilege is a choice
He's the shepherd of His sheep
And only we can hear His voice.

Trust

I've put my faith
In many things
But always end up burned
Praying, hoping things would change
You'd think
By now I would've learned
That people don't do
What they said they'll do
Knowing it's a must
Actions and words are separate
Tell me who to trust.

God or man
As I understand
Are the choices
One or two?
I've put my trust in the both of them
But only one has followed through
Within their words
I've often heard
The truth is there to see
But how is that,
Both have my back?
When only one could set me free.

I'll take my chance
And trust in God
For He is number one
And no person here, gone, far, or near
Can compete with what
He's done
His words alone
Sustain this world
And for that
His work is commendable
So, it is now
I trust in Him
For people
Are not dependable.

Church

The body of Christ is
Much more than a building
With steeples high
And fine art with gilding
Encrusted crosses
And spiritual things
Assigned seats, titles, tithes
And purity rings

The body is sacred
The body is healing
The truth in motion
The body is breathing
Life into the lives
Of those in their storm
Fighting
For the hearts
To be soon reborn
Living for God
Refusing to conform
To the world
We're the Gospel
In human form
On fire
With desire
Not to be lukewarm

Amara Kursha

Our souls transform
With a need to search
For lost souls in the sea
We are the living church
We aid to the sick, homeless
And healthy
Give hope to the broke, ugly
And wealthy
The message is the same
Now, tomorrow and then
We've comprehended
What's intended
And let the church say, Amen.

Come as You Are

Come all who are broken
Down and stressed
Come to Him
He'll give you rest
Those who thirst
And hunger too
Draw to Him
He'll draw to you
Sinners, saints and
In between
Bloody, dirty
And even clean
Hearts and souls
Truths and lies
Muted Lips
And blinded eyes
Deafened ears
Bitter tongues
Crushed bones
And blackened lungs
Struggle, pain
And disease
Standing up
Or on your knees
Doubts, fears, tears
And sweat

Amara Kursha

Old news
And new regret
Naked skin
Or Sunday's best
It doesn't matter
How you're dressed
Who you are
Or where you've been
Won't stop His love
So welcome in
Close enough
Or way too far
It doesn't matter
Just come as you are.

God's Waiting Room

Thicker than these walls
Is my anticipation
Time still moves
And I can feel
The perspiration
Leaking from my pores
There are no windows
Neither are there doors
Right above
An empty ceiling
Then below
An empty feeling
Shifting in my seat
Can my soul
Withstand the heat?
The heat of purification
In the end
A new creation
In this room
There's no debating
In His room
There's only waiting
And oftentimes
There's tears and whining
Through this process of refining
My faith is what's required

Amara Kursha

My trust is what's desired
As I'm tested through the fire
And He aims to take me higher
This place is just a blessing
It's His love that He's expressing
And behind these walls
Here lies my fate
So for my God,
It's here I'll wait.

Humanity

Oh, God
Oh, God
What will it take
To save these lives
For goodness sake
We're bleeding red
In seas of blue
Not one by one
But two by two
The pain is real
Here and abroad
People thinking that they
Could play God
And go unjudged
With no detection
They protect and serve
But only one complexion
Seems to only thrive
While it's a full-time job
Trying to stay alive
Black on Black
It's black and white
So wrong is wrong
And right is right
We should not fret
Or be afraid

Amara Kursha

For God is love
In every shade
But bodies pile
And numbers too
The question is now
What will we do?
An eye for an eye
Is not the plan
Divided we fall
Together we stand
If there's no change
It's just insanity
So let's all choose love
For the sake of humanity.

God Is…

God is...
My weakness
My innermost desired
Completeness
That indescribable
Undeniable feeling
My hope,
Purpose and meaning
He is
Better than
Publisher's Clearing House
Knocking on my door
Much greater than my
Desire to be rich
And my fear of being poor
He is beautiful
In every dimension
And did I mention
He is my rock
Solid and strong
I can't go wrong
With a father like that
Who's got my back
Constantly protecting me
Never neglecting me

Amara Kursha

God is...
Real
Not in the sense of a
Tangible feeling
But His presence is
Revealing
More and more
Of eternity
Beyond the eye can see
And He created me
Now I may not be your
Cup of tea
But I belong to Him
And He's within
Filling me up to the brim
With His truth spilling
And by faith I'm willing
To say that He is love
And He can do
Exceedingly
Abundantly
And above
Every thought
Or notion
Or person
He's King
He's exactly who
He is
God is everything.

My Best Friend

My Best Friend
Knows me like
The back of His hand
And though it was once
Pierced and blood-stained
That hand has held me
Pointed me to righteousness
Compelled me to greatness
Helped increase my faith
Turned my crooked
Road straight
And wait
Have I told you
That He's amazing
And that I can't
Help but find myself
Praising Him
Embracing Him
There's no
Replacing Him
His Father did a good thing
Raising Him
He's beyond therapeutic
He's the Prince of Peace

My Best Friend
Never holds me back
He truly knows me
Propelling me forward
Is His knack
He is freedom
His essence
And His name is sweet
Right now
We're long distance
But one day we'll meet
He's perfect in every way
Some think that
He's fictional
But He's so real
His love unconditional
I promise
If you knew Him
He would set you free
And I have a pretty good feeling
He died for you
Like He did for me.

Fear

My greatest enemy
Stalks my heart
Like a predator
Twists up my words
Like a
News line editor
Turns up the heat
Just to make
Me sweat
And makes me feel
Doubt, pain, hurt
And regret
With it
I always worry
While I fight to live
It tells me that I'm broke
While I fight to give
It makes me choke
It grows
With power
When I choose to feed it
Then it dictates my life
And tells me
That I need it

Amara Kursha

It's the reason I am behind
And my life is stressful
It's the only thing
Stopping me
From being successful
My God said
It's not in my DNA
So when "IT" comes around
I should
Stop and pray
For I have the power
Not this sinful spirit
And all it knows is lies
I refuse to hear it
So I'll look "IT" in its face
And I'll say it clear
With God,
I will have no fear.

Decisions, Decisions

When all the chips
Have fallen
And you're faced with
Something new
When all you have
Are questions
That surely question
What you thought you knew

When you're tired
Of this world
And in your flesh
There's no provision
You're free to make
A choice
The ultimate decision

Now your options
May be hard
But an answer
Is still demanded
Because the choices
You have made until now
Have left you stranded

Your future is at stake
And other lives
Can be impacted
It's now
You must be humble
And then your pride
Can be subtracted

This decision could
Change your life
And lighten the burden
Of your load
Generations may be altered
Way beyond
The fork in the road

I can tell you
I chose Jesus
And He changed my life
In every way
And if Jesus is your choice
I pray you choose
Him every day.

The Road to Righteousness

Fresh is the
Newly laid pavement.
The pathway to eternity;
A heavenly arrangement
Open to the willing
And yet traveled by a few
With a sign reading
"You can make it,
But the decisions' up to you"
A journey where you know
The outcome
And your final destination
A narrow road
Ever winding
With some spiritual restoration
An alley with dips
And valleys
Often darkened by reality
A passage led
With a peace
Stronger
Than any
Wicked principality
A trail with perfect
Bread crumbs,
Manna,

Truth,
And living water
The course
In which you become the clay
And then God becomes the potter
The route that's most
Unpopular
The lonely lane of
Joy and sorrow
The point at which
You block the world
And then Jesus is
Who you request to
Follow
The line of
Divine appointment
And the direction
Of His likeness
It starts with just a step
And a decision to be righteous.

To Die For

Who I am now
Is far from who I use to be
I aimed to please the world
But found the world
Had no use to me

I fell for every plot and ploy
Every trick and scheme
And traded all my worth
Just to boost my self-esteem

I fought my inner demons
With no faith or religion
Feeding into the devil
Decision after decision

Slipping into his ways
Doing what he demanded
Until I realized
I had broken every commandment

I ate forbidden fruit
And hid from my creator
Sin was not the motive
But I was the perpetrator

Amara Kursha

Then my eyes were opened
And I saw what is true
Jesus was near
And He was sent to save me too

He knew me, flaws and all
And my reputation
He knew I had given into sin, lust,
And every temptation

And He knew every inch
Of my life and more
Yet sacrificed His life
On the cross and bore

There took on my shame
From this life before
'Cause in His heart
He thought I was
Someone to die for.

Next Chapter

Life is like a book
And every vessel
Just a cover
Our truth is in the pages
And in the pages
You'll discover
A story about love
Between our God
And all creation
And how He sent His son
The only one
For our salvation
And how His blood
Is inked
In every passage
Of the story
And how His death
Was not the end
But just a glimpse
Into His glory
And how with
Every day
He sends
An open invitation
For freedom
In His name

Amara Kursha

To His eternal celebration
And how it's up to us
To accept or decline
The fate of that decision
Will be
Revealed over time
That the death
Of our sins
Is not the end
Instead it's just a factor
To moving on with our lives
To the next chapter.

www.ingramcontent.com/pod-product-compliance
Lightning Source LLC
Chambersburg PA
CBHW021132300426
44113CB00006B/391